Mommy Needs a Moment

Veronica Oddo

BookLeaf Publishing

India | USA | UK

Presentation by *BookLeaf Publishing*

Web: www.bookleafpub.com

E-mail: info@bookleafpub.com

ISBN: 9789358734089

First edition 2023

To My Creator,

My Origins,

My Soulmate,

And

My Sunshine.

ACKNOWLEDGEMENT

God,
You have blessed me with a divinely gifted family to prepare for the journey with.
Not a conventional family, but one connected in a way words fail to fully convey.
I wouldn't be where I am today if everything, both beautiful and ugly, hadn't happened exactly the way it did.
The presence of my people around me while both enduring and celebrating drives me to persevere.
I wouldn't want it any other way.
Thank you, Lord.

My Sunshine,
When you're my age, if you're feeling blue,
I want you to know it's okay. Mommy used to feel like that, too.
I hope that, you find peace in these words, knowing that you're never alone.
 I can share a special part of my heart with you, now that you're grown.

The part that shows how important you really are.

Without you, there is no way that I could have
made it this far.
Your smile lights up my world, with a joy that
must be felt.
Your eyes are filled with warmth that truly
makes me melt.

Through all of the chaos, and all of the sin,
Guiding you to be much better than I, drives me
to win.
Your pain is my pain. Your Joy is my Joy.
A copy of me, in my little boy.

Nothing compares to my love for you.
In all that you think, and all that you do.
Don't cry, my baby. You're never alone.
You'll always have mommy. Close to your heart,
like home.

PREFACE

I have had my fair share of life changing experiences, but being a mother has transformed me. My outlook on life has changed drastically. I've been blessed to have many beautiful moments planted in the garden of life and to have my son with me for those moments. While I'm trying to show him the pretty flowers, my hand quickly plucks weeds and scares the pests away without him seeing. The battle to maintain untouched innocence for as long as possible, before he's old enough that the world takes control out of my hands.

This collection of poetry is a journey that I've been on, and found many who have felt the same.

A reflection of the battle that parents have to go through, while they duel with their demons silently.

While trying to break generations worth of abuse and cycles, by creating healthy patterns for their children, parents have to fight their own internal programming. Parents have to be responsible for updating software they didn't ask for, and making sure that viruses don't infiltrate our own children.

This internal process isn't a gentle one, but it has to happen in silence.

We have to act as if this new, healthy way of thinking is how it's always been. As if we're experts. So that when our children look to us for guidance, they will feel secure. They will feel safe.

That safety net takes away their resistance to try and fly. It encourages them to be bold, and daring, knowing that someone safe is ready to catch them. Even if we don't execute perfectly, we just hope that we didn't repeat the same things done to us.

We create feelings of insecurity within ourselves, pressured about not being able to deliver on our new standards. Nothing will feel like we did good enough, from the heart of an abused person trying to be a parent.

We always feel like we fail.

We always feel like we fall short.

Even when we succeed, we doubt our success.

My son always brings me back to focus.
Wonderfully smart,
Beautifully confident,
Emotionally intelligent,
And caring beyond belief.

I don't want to distract him from his potential, having to watch out for his Mama.

This collection is straight from a meeting of my inner demons and angels.
They've sat together, throwing my emotions and reasoning back and forth like a game of table tennis. I've been left in thought with only those arguments to listen to.
The result, a vulnerable collection of poetry. Hopefully someone battling themselves will read it and know that they are not alone.
I hope it speaks to a part of you that you may be scared to listen to.
I hope that you find comfort in knowing that behind every put together parent, there is likely a battle raging within them, as there is you and I.
It's okay to lose the battle.
You won't lose the war.

The war within is won with Love.

Tempting Tendrils

Finger's decorated with gentle lace strands.
So enticing. Magnetic.
Smooth and featherlight to the eye, promising
sweet comfort.
Deceived by appearance.
Instead, the viscid surface clings to the digits of
the allured victim.

Lacing transforms to chains.
Where intricacies wind together so complex that
the prey struggles to escape.
Finger's dance and pull the mesh, attached to
another's flesh.
Where beautiful billows once flowed, locks
latched tight took their place.
Master's fingers toy with strands of control
adhered firmly to the foundation.

All while the other hand calmly taunts.
Flagrantly fiddling the key, just out of grasp.

Muted Melodies

My heart sings the song of truth.
The voices whisper the discord of doubt.
In blindness, I find bliss.
The voices fade into static, while the ballad
plays louder.

My heart sings the song of truth.
When the elation and ecstasy could carry you
through valleys without rest.
When there's no room for reality or reason.
The voices whisper the discord of doubt.

The orchestra of honesty is permeating through
my soul.
The cacophony of chaos is smothered,
Unable to project in a room filled with harmony.

When my heart sings the song of truth, doubt is
drowned out.
Every discontentment lost in the melody.

Diligent Delusion

Profound statements,
Created by articulate minds.

Was an influential thought even spoken aloud if
only ears of ignorance are around to hear it?

Reality reverberates off of the delusion.
Ricocheting, silently.
The fortress of insanity, built reinforced with
righteousness.

Sturdy, to withstand the power of candor.
Sound proof, to muffle the voices of reason.

Thin air

A voice that is fast to bellow.
An anger that is quick to join the occasion.
A rage that can catch fire like kindling, with no
water in sight.

The expectations, high as clouds.
The pressure to soar weighs heavy.
The wings of an eagle held firmly in place, by
the monstrous feet of the elephant.
No space to spread wide, and feel the wind
caress your feathers.

Your wings furiously flap.
Fighting the weights and the heat.
Through billows of smoke, dripping in lead
chains,
You reached heights that were once just a myth.

Mountain Top Kingdom

A place like Home.
>High in the mountains, beyond the reach
of routine.
>A kingdom, in the clouds.

>Crystal clear streams flow like veins
through the rock.
>The cool, clean water gives life to Your
creatures.

>Vibrant Vegetation grows abundantly at
the steams edge.
>Flourishing Flowers, all decorated in
Brilliant Butterflies.
>A Picture of Peace.

>From atop the mountain, the rawness of
the world can be seen.
>The way that He made it.
>The purity of its natural state.

>Sitting in Solitude,
>Surrounded in Serenity,
>My Soul Sings.

A wishful whisper,
To be Seen;
Heard;
Understood.

A Boisterous Bellow, Boldly declares,
"I am here, Child".

Constellations of Comfort

A void, filled with concentrated darkness.

A strange sensation, gradually noticeable.
A small burning.
The warmth of a single light.

Glowing red, creating a heat never experienced
before.
Impossible to ignore.
The new sensation drew the focus to it with a
painful hunger.

The more attention it absorbed, the hotter the
flame became.
The energy of the light grew so compelling, it
shifted from red to blue.

All the suffering was all made miniscule as the
light took control.
The star ignited torment, and soothed the
wounds.

The blue engulfed the empty space, finding long
forgotten corners.

To the bewilderment of the chasm, it was
showered in contentment, rather than
discomfort.

The blue soothed the hollow, dim sky.
Its power was so concentrated, it could not be
repressed.
The light overtook the darkness.
A single star erupted into a million.

A vast plain of dark transformed.
The void, speckled with white.
Finally, a sky full of stars.

Fallen Oaks

When a tree that used to shelter you, topples down.

The Sturdy Oak that held your hand while you explored its heights.
The Towering Pine that cast shade and rained seeds of imagination.
The Unwavering Palm, dipped in salt and sand.

When the seemingly immortal, fall.

The ground welcomes the wood back into the cycle, while your heart breaks. The empty spaces where roots ran deep feeling the loneliness.

Mother's Magic

Mundane moments you made special.
Things that surely didn't deserve long nights and
lost sleep.
You endured the dark circles and groggy
mornings, for me.

Hours of effort in exchange for minutes of
enjoyment.
My mind, not able to even fully understand the
cost.
My eyes are open now.
I can see your reasons.
Why the meticulous wrapping on the presents
under the tree creates the magic of the holiday.
Why every card you create is personalized and
time stamped.
Why it's worth the rest and the time.

A Girl Scout, a scientist, artist, veterinarian,
cheerleader.
Anything you had to be for me, you became.
Now I get to be the shape shifter.

Not an easy task,
But I had a good role model.

Gardener of Good

Sifting soft soil with your delicate fingers.
Pink petals piled up from a wilted bud.
Cautious, careful cleanup near our sharper
friend, the cactus.

More mommy moments while we create a
display of growth.
An unlikely array of plants, with bases tightly
intertwined.
Velvety leaves, vibrant colors, bright blooms.
Towering tall is the thin spikes of the garden
guard.

Our love pours as we clean and turn the piece of
Earth.
The roots strengthen with our nourishment.
My heart warms in euphoria.
Watching your kind hands create good so
naturally.

The garden, my heart, is soothed by your
extraordinary existence.

Uniform

Cotton, nylon, spandex.
Load after load,
Meticulously folding.
Pinching off any fibers,
Ironing every wrinkle.
Lining up the corners on the tiny plastic hangers.
As soon as I'm finished, the tower seems to have
reappeared.
Smeared in mud.
Coated in crumbs.
Stains set firm,
With no help in sight, aside from bleach.
Hangers long discarded, and the only destination
for these dressings is back into the cycle.

And

I'd pinch every fiber,
Fold just as specifically,
And leave every piece scented like home, even
knowing it's going to come back tattered.

Because I also know, my life is beyond blessed
to be the person who removes the debris,
While I listen to you revel in the experiences
that dress your soul in the feeling of adventure

The Laughter in Living

The silly joke that you couldn't finish telling me without erupting into giggles.

The shy smile that creeps out when you get a surprise, followed by energetic chuckles.

Sleep deprivation brings an uncensored, purely hilarious, version of laughter.

Everything entraps you in a spiral of gut busting bellows.

My favorite part;

Being the audience that you want to share your joy with, and getting to see you light up with pride when I react.

Seeing your dimples pinch the apples of your cheeks when you grin, right where mine do.

Putting your giddy mind to rest at the end of a strenuous day of exploration, in preparation for the next day full of giggles.

Sleep Soft as Silk

Your soft features grow softer,
As the comfort of cuddles cleans the day
from your mind.
I hold you close to my heart, as you
grow heavier and higher.

Enveloped in blankets, you cure my
exhaustion. You bring me to rest.
Soft melodies float within our walls.
Creating serenity.

I can feel my eyelids slipping closed
with yours.
The crickets chirp, while you turn to
burrow into my arms.
Hearts touching, I cradle you into a
cloud of sleep with me.
Sweet dreams broadcasted into both of
our resting minds.

Muddy Mascara

Dreaming of what I've lost, tears run down my
cheeks.
Staining them in salt.

My lashes weighed down with mascara and
misery.
Trying to clear away the beads of sadness.

My vision blurs, as the droplets collect into an
ocean.
Vast enough I can feel myself drowning.

Once the barrier breaks,
The furious fluttering from my lashes has no
hope to hold back the waters.

Good Morning

The cool veil of quiet that coats the morning air.
insects and creatures softly whisper their songs
through the dark.
I rise before the day once more.
The clock says morning, but the stars still hang
in the sky.
The muted beams of sunlight dance over the
horizon, while the moon races to hide before the
sun's arrival.
With the moon's disappearance, the black drains
from the sky.
Paint strokes from above decorate the fresh day
in colors.
With every passing second, the pigments shift
and mix,
Blending yesterday into today.

Fumbling to Finish

Time is running a race, and I can't keep up.
        The starting flag cut through the air, my
body unable to find movement.

Unforgiving ground reaches up to envelop me.
Pulling my lead weights down and tethering
them in place.
Muted.

Every fiber is screaming, in silence.
The pleas dying behind closed lips.
Unspoken words reverberated. Piled up high,
until there's no room for even sweet nothings to
escape and find sound.

The surface tries to take ahold of me,
But my purpose propels me forward.

The race moved at the speed of chaos,
A fuse lit at both ends.

Where most would panic, I had to protect.
I am responsible for a precious package to be
delivered to the finish line.
The goal appears to be ever moving.

Where I once carried you, your legs have grown
to carry themselves.
You're fast enough to beat me at this race now.

You still slow to a trot,
And come hold my hand,
        So we can finish as a team.

My Only Sunshine

Attached at my hip,
You just want to be close.

My heart, once your neighbor, is a safe space for
you.
Cuddling on sick days, fighting away bad
dreams,
I'm lucky to be here for all the in-betweens.

The questions and discoveries about life and its
wonders.
To protect yourself from bad guys, bullies, and
enemies of your bubble.
To stop and marvel at the majesty of even the
smallest things.
Sharing moments that bring a forgotten lense of
purity to perspective.

When I knew I'd have you,
I had no idea what to do.

How to make sure you didn't know what
struggle felt like.
How to let you explore yourself and guide you.
How to nurture a piece of my heart.

An independent sliver.

Never could I have fathomed transformation so
profound.
My reason, my purpose, rewritten.

The honey gold warmth that flows through your
eyes, full and innocent.
Framed in smile lines, gently creasing your
untarnished skin.

You are a ray of sunshine so powerful, so potent.
Even the most dense rain clouds evaporate in
your path.

Background

Is this okay?
	To feel?
	To think?
	To move?

	Who am I even asking?
	You?
My Creator?
	Myself?

	Permission grants me an incomparable
serenity.
	To be secure enough to validate your
own existence is a myth in my mind.
	Only with the permission of the world,
and all of its occupants, do I find contentment in
my space.

	The shadow days are a distant memory.
	Of being a whisper.
	Of being transparent, a ghost in plain
sight.
	Of being clay, molded by whatever
hands are able to grab ahold of me.

When the sun sets,
When my bed and my thoughts are the
only things keeping me company,
No longer can I justify the darkness.
It's time to turn on the spotlight.

Swimming with Saints

The ocean crashed on the shore, with ferocity.
White foam sprayed where the water smashed
into the sand.
Driven by the instability of the foreboding
clouds above us.
Threatening to unleash downpour, rumbling
faintly in the distance.

The sea was churning, creating a vortex of foam
and sand.
A salty murkiness that my eyes couldn't
penetrate.
The force of the waves jostled me with every
step.
But through the waves, without sight, I carried
myself into the sea to meet You.

The hand of another who knows you're near,
guides me under the surface.
Straight into the face of adversity.

Time functioned outside of reality.
Frigid water instead felt like fire, but dimmer.
Like a bath of the softest, most potent light.

Where the warmth touched, sparks simmered
across the surface.
Skin enveloped in flames, an even brighter light
surrounded me.
A feeling of security, the gentle pressure of an
embrace.
Comfort.

The bubble evaporates, as my lungs stretch to
breathe.
The warmth still clings, with a furiosity felt
deep.
A golden cloak of protection, gently draped
around me.

Soul Sister

The base of our connection, a low consistent
beat.
The foundation of our energy, a deep steady
rhythm.
The sense of grounding, held sturdy in the
sound.
The profound impression of safety, surrounded
by the melodies.

Thank you,
 for being that sense of security, with no concern
for miles or minutes.
Thank you,
  for being a reliable, trustworthy ear to share my
thoughts and tears with.
Thank you,
 for being an immovable wall, guarding from the
lurking adversaries.

The harmony of our vibrations humming.
The calm of completion.
The synchronization of our souls.

You care in a way that makes me value myself.

You fit perfectly in a space I've never been able
to fill.
Your love is like the warmth of a perfect
morning breakfast together.
Your voice completes my sentences before my
lips even twitch.

When we're building together, the brick bonds
stronger.
The strength of the stone intensified.
Where our castles crumbled alone, they tower
together.
Touching heights we only used to dream of.

Doors Left Open

I only have to obey.
     You know the way.

     When there's hundreds of doors,
thousands of keys,
     You place an arrow where only my eyes
can see.

     The bolt unfastened, propped ajar.
     Glistening beams call out from afar.

     PSSTTT!

     A thought, not my own, takes stage in
my mind.
     "Come closer, my Child. Your purpose,
you'll find.

     Do not doubt what you hear,
I will always appear.
When you call out to plea,
And shout with glee.
When you're lost on the road,
Mind ready to explode,

I will lead."

       The door, now spread wide,
Calls me inside.
Promising peace.
Relaxing Release.

To feel divine favor,
From my mighty savior.

The War Within

I thank you for the hills, the obstacles, the fire,
the confusion.
I thank you for giving me more than I thought I
could handle.
I thank you for the pressure, the darkness, the
isolation.
I thank you for taking me through the most
treacherous waters.

In all those moments, I had to learn.
How to put out the fire, or use it for light.
How to rest in the darkness, under Your
protection.
How to craft a vessel durable enough to fight the
waves.

You guide me across minefields, tending to
every step.
You speak sense to me, barely above a whisper,
asking for my attention.
You give me what would appear to the eye as
luck, but to the aware heart, a blessing.

My colorful history, setting a foundation of
knowledge.

My present safety, knowing I have a place to call
home.
My future potential, inspiration flying right
under the surface of the clouds,
About to soar high.

You have prepared me, protected me, and
provided me with opportunities for new
chapters.
The battle has subsided, but the war never ends.

To withstand,
Love must be nurtured.
For your family, for your higher power, for your
fortunes.
Most importantly,
Find love for yourself.